# LEGO STAR WARS

# OFFICIAL ANNUAL 2020

Match the missing pieces with the X-wing.

A B C D E

WHEEEEEE!

Which shadow belongs to Biggs?

A B C

Which symbol only appears once below?

Find the ships that are parked in the same order as the ones in the frame.

**A**

**B**

**C**

Who did Luke and his friends disguise themselves as? Work out who the heroes are and connect them with their disguises.

1  2  3  4  5

Count the helmets, blasters and fire extinguishers and circle the correct total for each one.

| 5 | 4 | 4 |
| 6 | 6 | 7 |
| 8 | 8 | 6 |

Which droid should appear at the end of each sequence?

A    B    C    D

1

2

3

Learn how to draw C-3PO with this step-by-step guide.

SORRY, ARTOO, YOU STILL HAVE SOME PRACTISING TO DO.

13

# ALWAYS READ THE MANUAL

FASTER, FASTER! I CAN'T WAIT TO JOIN THE REBELS. I WANT TO FIGHT THE EMPIRE WITH THEM!

TAKE IT EASY, LUKE. WE'RE ALMOST THERE.

AT THE FAR END OF THE GALAXY, A GROUP OF YOUNG HEROES ARRIVE AT THE SECRET BASE OF THE REBEL ALLIANCE ...

WAIT! I THINK THAT'S AN OLD FRIEND OF MINE FROM TATOOINE!

BIGGS! IS THAT YOU? AM I GLAD TO SEE YOU, BUDDY!

LUKE? SO, YOU'VE FINALLY LEFT THAT SANDPIT ON TATOOINE, PAL. GREAT! WANNA CHECK OUT THE COOL FIGHTERS WE HAVE HERE?

HERE'S A T-65B X-WING FIGHTER. IT'S FASTER, MORE STURDY AND HAS MORE FIRE POWER THAN THE IMPERIAL TIE FIGHTERS ...

... BUT IT'S NOT EASY TO FLY AND EVERY PILOT HAS TO LEARN THE MANUAL BY HEART.

WOW! IT'S AWESOME! COULD I JUST SIT IN THE COCKPIT FOR A BIT?

Match the rebel pilots with their descriptions.

A. He's the only pilot sporting a dark grey helmet.

B. He's wearing white gloves and holding a blaster.

C. You'll recognize him from his light brown beard.

D. No other pilot has a black moustache like him.

E. He may look stern, but he's not.

BIGGS DARKLIGHTER

JEK PORKINS

DUTCH VANDER

ZEV SENESCA

WEDGE ANTILLES

Connect the identical ships into pairs.

Circle a character that stands out from the others in each group.

Connect the dots and help Luke regenerate inside the bacta tank.

WHO WANTS A CUPCAKE?
PLEASE SAY NOW! LUKE? NO?
OK, I'LL EAT IT THEN.

Find the rebel groups shown below in the crowds.

Which way should Han go to escape Boba Fett and reach the *Millennium Falcon*?

MILLENNIUM FALCON

A   B   C

Mark all the parts, seen on the screen, that Chewbacca needs to take out of the *Falcon*.

ALL RIGHT, CHEWIE, GET TO WORK AND I'LL GO GRAB SOMETHING TO EAT.

Use the code to colour in the picture and find out who the previous owner of the *Millennium Falcon* was.

Untangle the lines and find out who the pilot of each fighter is.

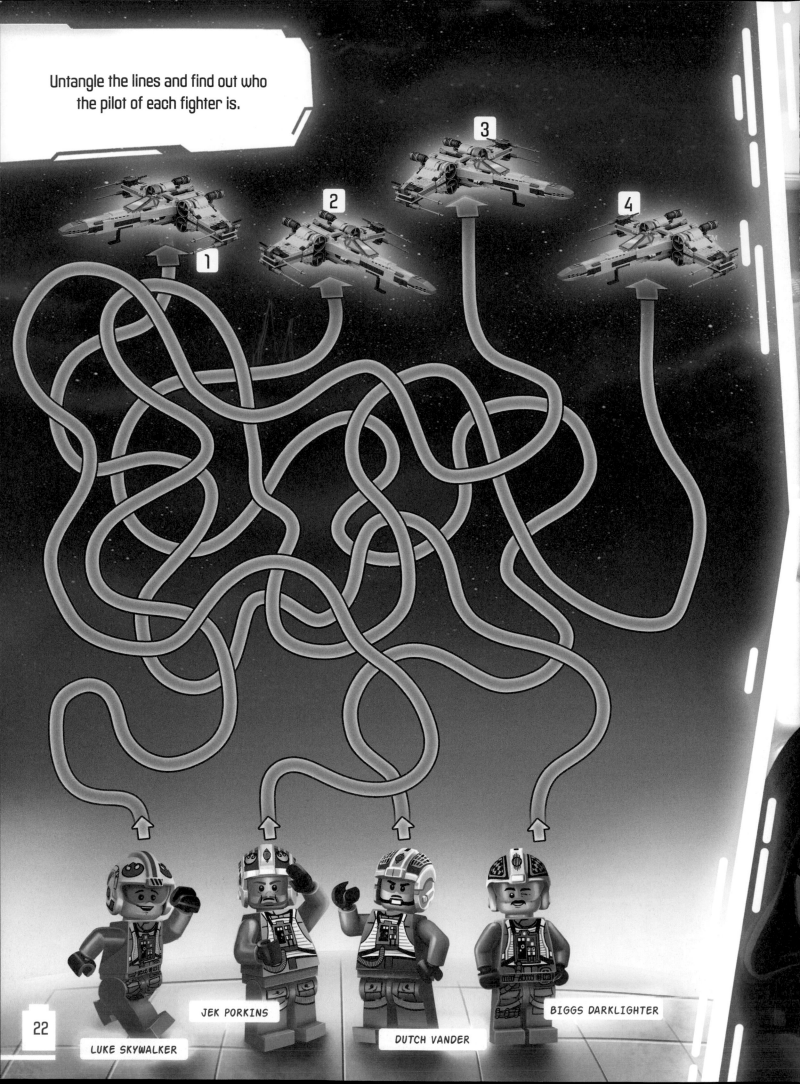

1

2

3

4

JEK PORKINS

BIGGS DARKLIGHTER

DUTCH VANDER

LUKE SKYWALKER

# A TRAP DETECTOR

MANY YEARS AFTER THE FALL OF THE EVIL EMPIRE, THE BRAVE REBEL HEROES ARE GATHERING FORCES AGAINST A NEW GALACTIC MENACE - THE CRUSHING POWER OF THE FIRST ORDER ...

EXCUSE ME, ADMIRAL. THE WHOLE RESISTANCE FLEET IS WAITING FOR YOUR INSTRUCTIONS ...

PATIENCE, THREEPIO. THE DETECTOR IS ALMOST FINISHED. IF IT WORKS, NO REBEL WILL EVER FALL INTO AN ENEMY TRAP AGAIN!

OH, THAT WOULD BE PERFECT, ADMIRAL. I HATE TRAPS!

YUB, NUB!

ON ENDOR FOR INSTANCE, I THOUGHT I'D BE EATEN ALIVE! LUCKILY, THE FEISTY EWOKS CHANGED THEIR MINDS AND HELPED US FIGHT THE EMPIRE ...

Connect the numbered black dots. Done?
Now do the same with the orange dots.

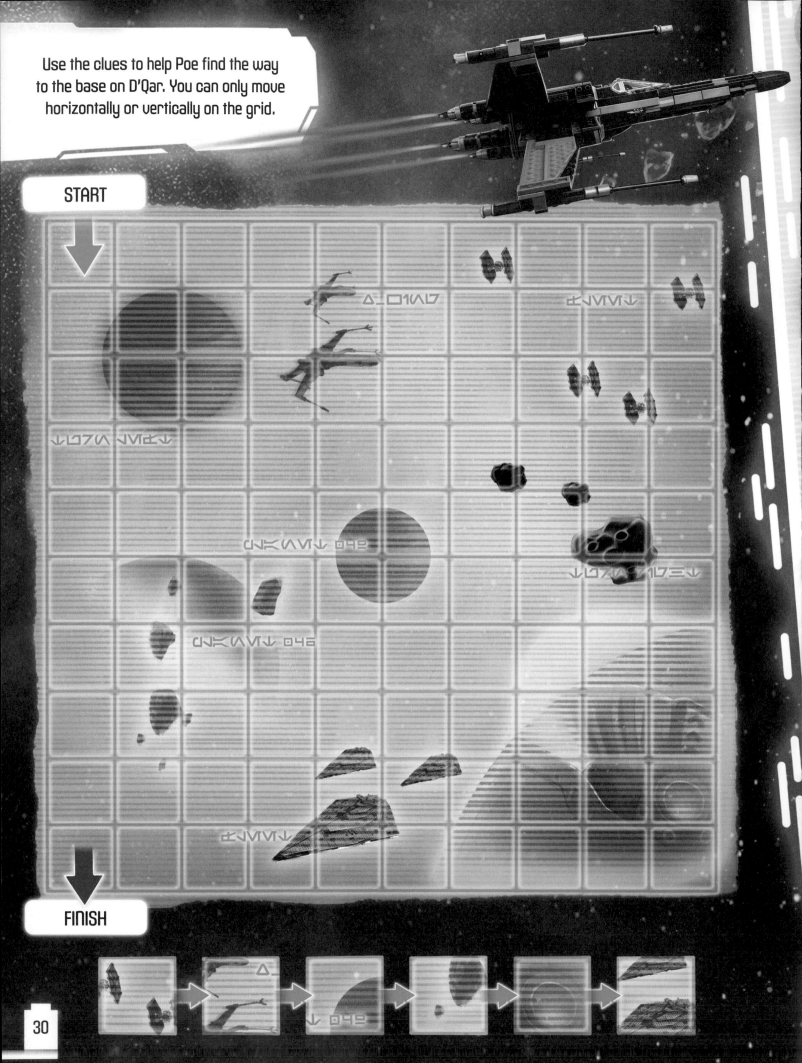

Use the clues to help Poe find the way to the base on D'Qar. You can only move horizontally or vertically on the grid.

START

FINISH

30

Which picture shows exactly the same pilot?

D

E

A

B

C

Colour in the fields where the Resistance should place its laser turrets. The numbers indicate how many of them should appear in each row and column.

WE NEED ORDER! AHEM ... BUT NOT THE 'FIRST ORDER' OF COURSE!

|  | 2 | 1 | 3 | 1 |
|---|---|---|---|---|
| 2 |  |  |  |  |
| 2 |  |  |  |  |
| 1 |  |  |  |  |
| 2 |  |  |  |  |

31

Match the loose parts to the right ships.

1

2

3

4

Connect 3 pairs of identical symbols with straight lines. The point where they cross will tell you who Vice Admiral Holdo will send on a mission.

EENY, MEENY, MINY, MO ...

Which way can BB-8 roll to reach C-3PO?

START

FINISH

Which picture fragments can you find
in the big scene?

1

2

3

4

5

Find the shadow that matches the Resistance's ski speeder.

A

B

C

YOU'LL NEVER GET MY PIZZA!

Untangle the blaster trajectories and mark what the X-wing has hit.

1

2

3

A

B

C

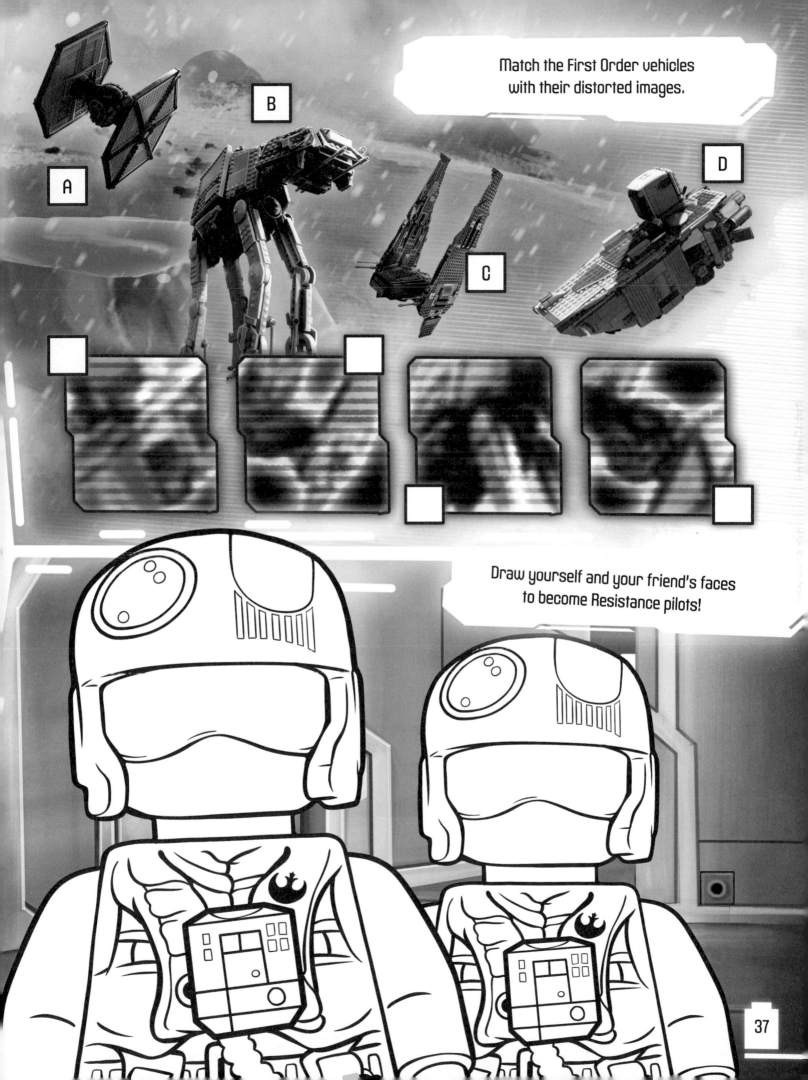

Match the First Order vehicles with their distorted images.

Draw yourself and your friend's faces to become Resistance pilots!

37

Number the ship crews 1-4, with 1 being the smallest team and 4 being the largest.

ROOAAARGH?

Find all the bricks the Resistance mechanic needs in the pile of parts.

I'M CURRENTLY ASSEMBLING AN X-WING. BUT WITH ALL THOSE BRICKS, I'LL HAVE ENOUGH TO BUILD TWO SCOOTERS AS WELL!

A     B     C     D

Arrange the porgs so that none of them will repeat in any row or column.

A B C D E

Which helmets should appear in the empty spaces?

NICE! BUT NOW THERE'S NO SPACE FOR MY HELMET!

Find 5 stormtroopers inside the crowded cantina.

I'VE BEEN LOOKING FOR THEM FOR 3 HOURS, AND HERE THEY ARE, DRINKING TEA ...

**RECRUITMENT EFFORTS**

IN A SECRET BASE OF THE RESISTANCE, THE BRAVE FIGHTERS FOR FREEDOM AND JUSTICE IN THE GALAXY ARE PREPARING FOR AN IMMINENT ATTACK OF THE SINISTER FIRST ORDER ...

... I KNOW, THREEPIO, THAT'S WHY I ORDERED THE NEW STARSHIPS. NOW WE'VE GOT MORE FIGHTERS AND BOMBERS THAN CREWS TO FLY THEM.

I AM PERFECTLY AWARE OF THAT, PRINCESS - I MEAN - GENERAL LEIA. THAT'S WHY WE HAVE ...

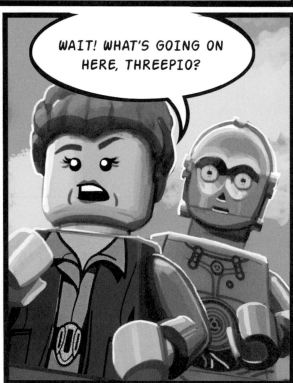

WAIT! WHAT'S GOING ON HERE, THREEPIO?

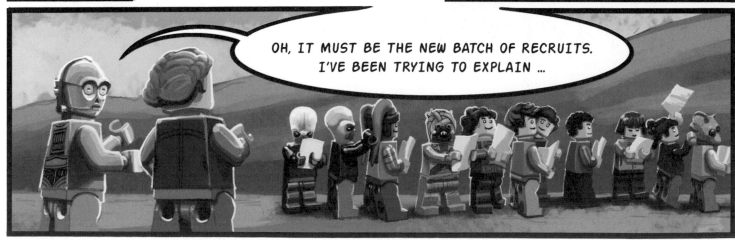

OH, IT MUST BE THE NEW BATCH OF RECRUITS. I'VE BEEN TRYING TO EXPLAIN ...

WE PUT UP NEW RECRUITMENT POSTERS RECENTLY.

IT LOOKS LIKE THEY'VE BEEN A SUCCESS!

BUT HOW MANY OF THE NEW RECRUITS ARE GOOD PILOTS?

NEVER MIND. WE'LL TRAIN THEM.

LOOK OVER THERE! POE DAMERON, THE BEST PILOT IN THE RESISTANCE, IS ALREADY ON THE JOB!

WELCOME TO THE RESISTANCE FLEET!

FLEET? WHAT FLEET? I'M JUST HERE FOR AN AUTOGRAPH!

Find 10 differences between these two scenes from the snow battle.

Find 6 Resistance symbols in one of the scenes on the page opposite.

Which pieces are part of the picture?

1

2

3

4

5

6

Combine the lines next to each character to make the symbols, and find everyone's location on the destroyer's deck.

Colour in the Resistance transport using the coloured dots.

IT LOOKS MUCH BETTER IN COLOUR!

Lead the friends back to base. Each can only move on fields with their assigned symbol.

Connect the identical droids into pairs.

LOTS OF FRIENDS FOR BB-8!

Look very closely at these pictures for 60 seconds.
Then turn over the page.

What pictures appeared on the previous page?
Remember: no peeking!

Check how well you did. Colour in the porgs
for every picture you get right.

Match the picture pieces to the big picture.

1

2

3

4

5

The villain whose portrait appears the most will soon be causing trouble for the Resistance heroes. Who is it?

Colour in the spaces marked with an X to reveal the X-wing's shadow. Which ship does it belong to?

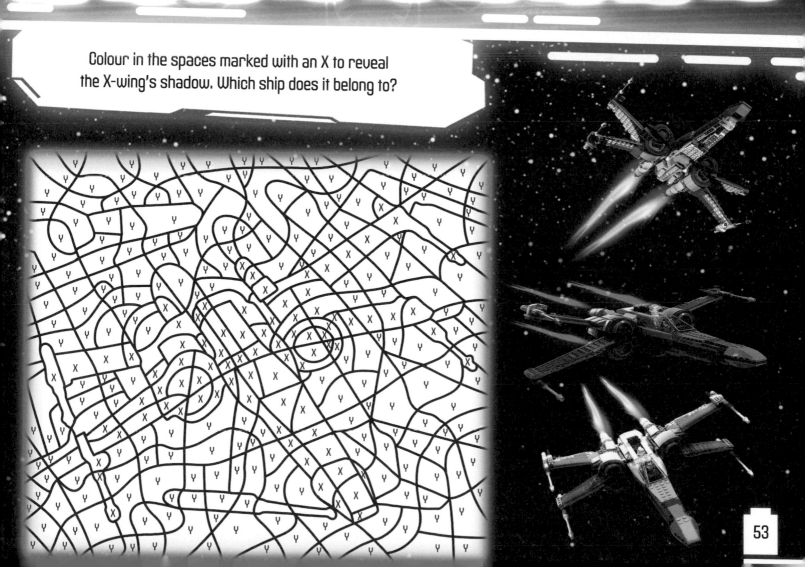

Cross out all the symbols and sequences shown below. The symbols left will reveal the code needed to start the ski speeder.

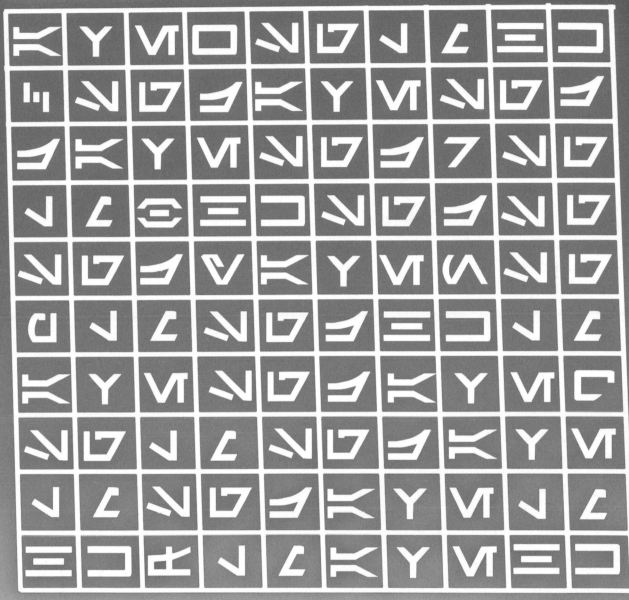

CODE:

How many blasters will you find in the Resistance armoury?

I'M SEEING DOUBLE ... NO, TRIPLE! QUADRUPLE! HELP!

Lead Kylo to his meeting with Luke Skywalker. The path must go through discs that share one of their two colours.

START

FINISH

HELLO, MY FORMER STUDENT. I SEE YOU GREW UP ... HMM, DID YOU CUT YOURSELF SHAVING?

Colour in the given number of fields in each row to find out what Chewbacca is thinking about.

Find a mistake on each one of Kylo Ren's portraits.

HURRY UP, TROOPER! MY FACE IS ALREADY GOING NUMB!

# ANSWERS

p. 5

p. 5

p. 6

p. 6

C

p. 8

1  3  2  4

1  3  2

4

p. 7

p. 8

p. 9

p. 10

1
2
3
4
5

p. 11

6  8  7

p. 16

A – Zev Senesca
B – Wedge Antilles
C – Jek Porkins
D – Biggs Darklighter
E – Dutch Vander

p. 11

p. 12

C

1  B

A

2  A

D

3  D

B

p. 17

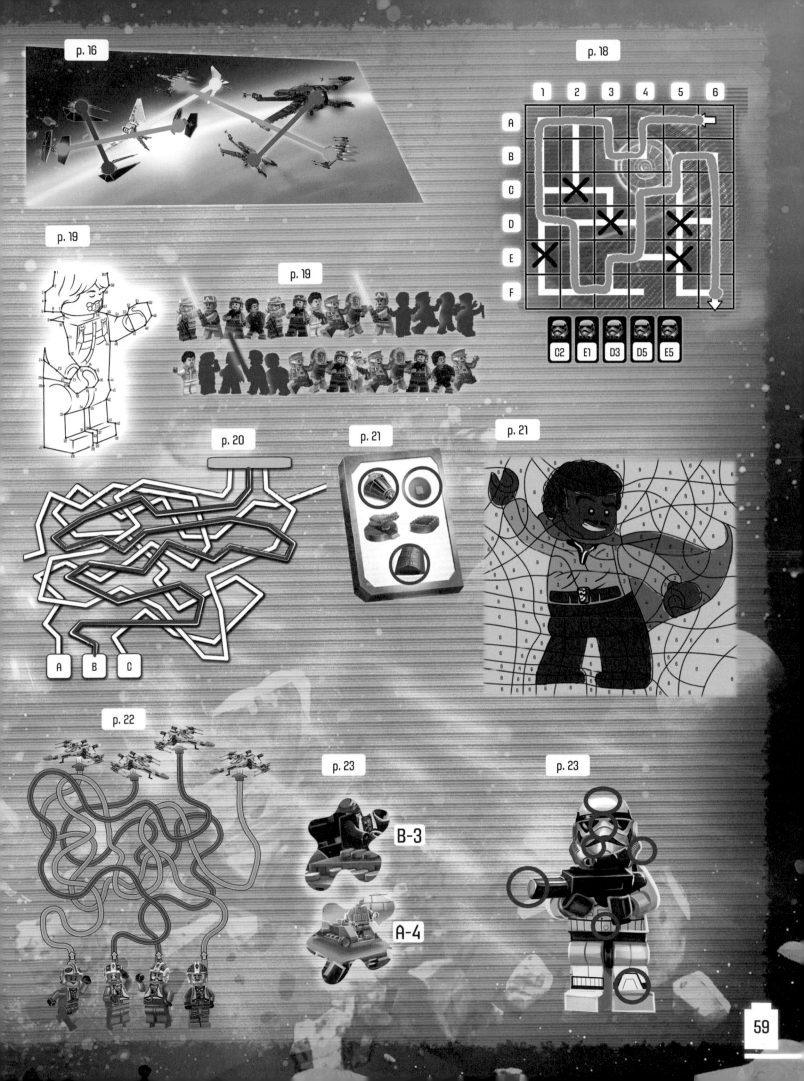

p. 16

p. 18

1  2  3  4  5  6

A
B
C
D
E
F

C2  E1  D3  D5  E5

p. 19

p. 19

p. 20

A  B  C

p. 21

p. 21

p. 22

p. 23

B-3

A-4

p. 23

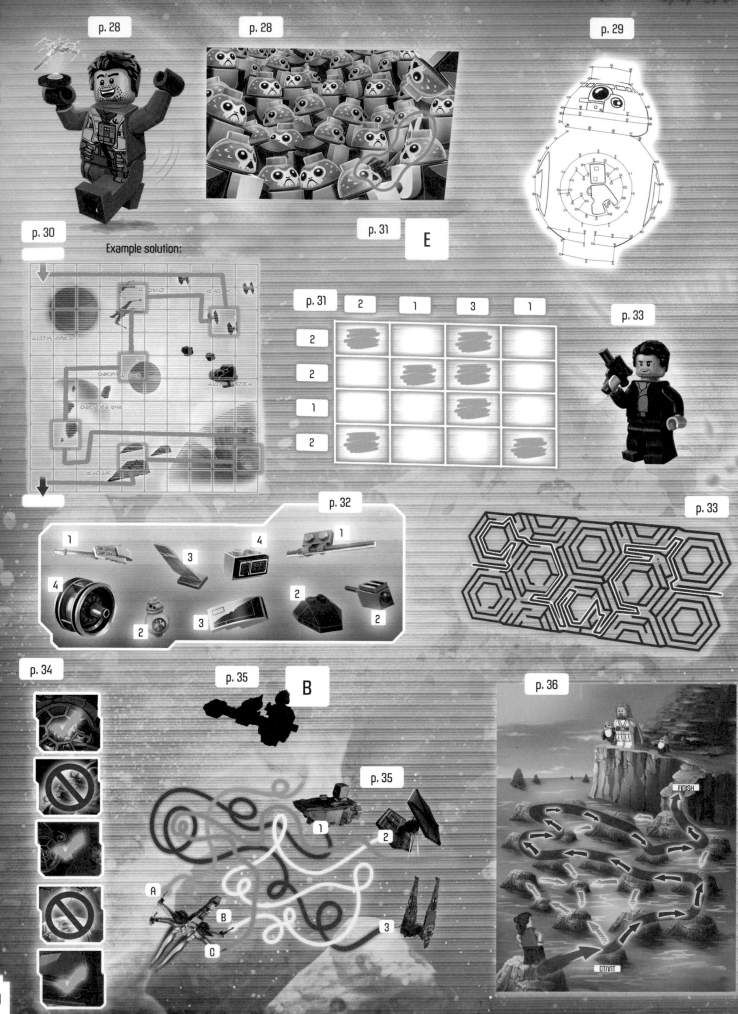

p. 28

p. 28

p. 29

p. 30

Example solution:

p. 31

E

p. 31

| | 2 | 1 | 3 | 1 |
|---|---|---|---|---|
| 2 | | | | |
| 2 | | | | |
| 1 | | | | |
| 2 | | | | |

p. 33

p. 32

1
3
1
4
4
2
2
2
3
2
2

p. 33

p. 34

p. 35

B

p. 36

FINISH

p. 35

1
2
3

A
B
C

START

p. 37

D  C

B  A

p. 38

p. 39

| | | 2 | 1 |
| 2 | | 4 | |
| 3 | | 2 | 4 |
| | 4 | 3 | |

p. 38–39

1    2    3    4

p. 41

B

E

A

B    D

p. 41

p. 40

p. 44–45

p. 45

p. 46

p. 46

p. 48

p. 49

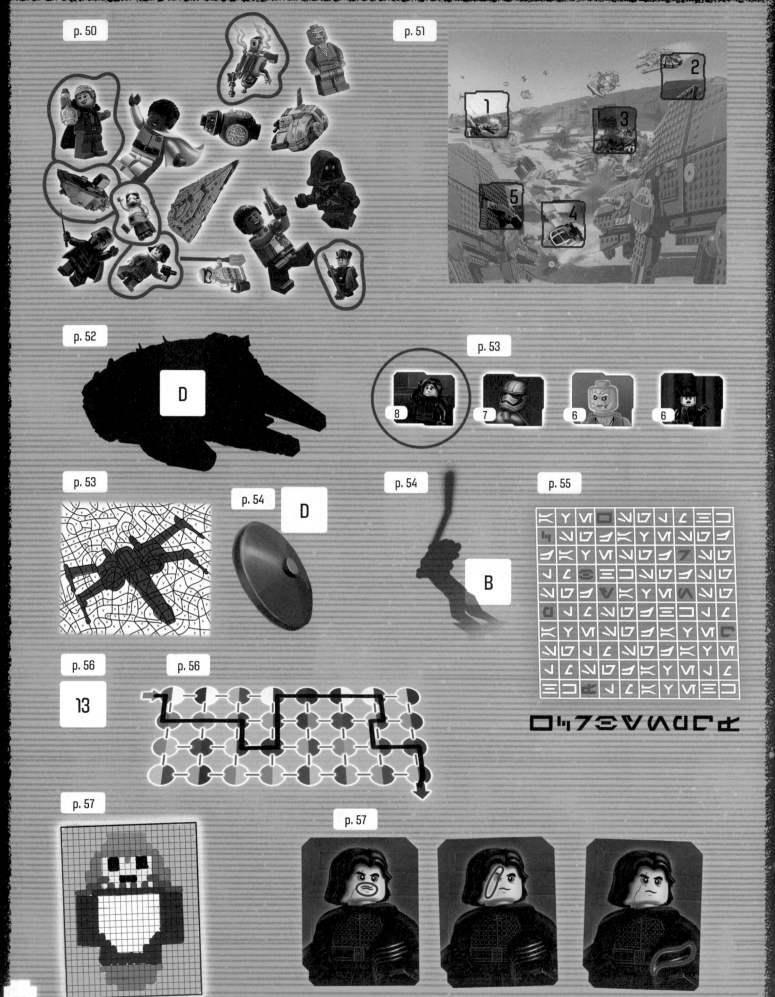

p. 50

p. 51

p. 52

D

p. 53

8  7  6  6

p. 53

p. 54

D

p. 54

B

p. 55

p. 56

13

p. 56

p. 57

p. 57